The political economy of tango in the 21ˢᵗ Century

Richard Schwartz

The political economy of tango in the 21ˢᵗ Century

© Richard Schwartz

First edition 2021

ISBN: 978-1-913329-39-6

Published by Dempsey & Windle
under their VOLE imprint

15 Rosetrees
Guildford
Surrey
GU1 2HS
UK
01483 571164
dempseyandwindle.com

British Library Cataloguing-in-Publication Data:
A catalogue record for this book is available from the British Library.

Cover photographs ©Lisa Neidich

Printed and bound in the UK

For Lisa, Ethan and Eliana

Poems

They held hands	9
National Lottery	10
JJS z"l	11
The oldest hatred	12
Inventory	13
Coffee united	14
Last word	15
Sulphur	16
My room	17
We have no names	18
Hello!	19
In time	20
At the end of the day	21
A day can turn on a dime	22
Reconciliation	23
A father's advice	24
Common assumption	25
Uncompleted Kaddish	26
The music of trees	27
Back in the day	28
Sometimes	29
Missing	30
Who knows One?	31
While	32
Daily	33
The impact of public holidays on productivity in the United Kingdom	34

Nearer   35
Restoration   36
Do you   37
Someone wrote a book   38
Instruments are not my friends   39
Zimbabwe dreaming   40
How long is a piece of string?   41
Lazy   42
Weather report   43
Eye to eye   44
Surprising what we get used to   45
As a general rule, I don't write about writing but 46
Memory's antibodies   47
Reckonings   48
Hamlet's masterclass   49
A divine response to theodicy (haiku)   50
History of the jigsaw   51
August   52
What next?   53
This is what it must be like   54
Why must the sky be blue?   55
Out of shape   56
9/2020   57
Being dark outside   58
Glory be   59
Faded ink   60

Missing in action   61
Days   62
Why when staring out   63
Phrases that have recently fallen into disuse   64
Zimbabwean cento   65
From what I can see   66
Not long ago   67
Out the window   68
At this time of year   69
The political economy of tango in the 21st Century   70
Contractors to the Council   71
I don't want to spoil your day, but...   72
The butcher (found poem)   73
Abraham   74

They held hands

Feeling unsafe in a strange part of town
they held hands, through the movie he
hated and she loved, they held hands.

As conflict loomed, they held hands,
below deck they held hands and on
the bridge, rocked in choppy seas.

Across the road, they held hands,
before the first note, held hands
maestro tapping at the podium.

They hid by the bottlebrush
tree, holding hands, by the
fence too, wanting repair.

They held hands when
teacher said to, tight
till their fingers hurt.

Eyes locked, hand
in hand, hobbling,
leaping centuries.

National Lottery

Not sure Aristotle would have shelled out
for a ticket; even less Maimonides, Gödel
or Aquinas. I'm guessing Averroes would
have given it a pass; thoughtful folk they
were, mindful of a universe that begs for
contemplation, avoiding the cacophony
of fifty-seven million, two hundred and
a couple more, give or take, semi-half-
believers bargaining respectfully with
God.

JJS z"l

In just a few weeks, he'd have made
ninety-seven, toasted with a whisky,
most likely Red Label, and, blood
sugar tested, a small slice of cake.
Instead he fell short by years, his
sudden collapse at the back of
the queue, head to the hard
cafe floor, startling staff and
patrons alike, not really his
nature to make a palaver.

An ambulance arrived, its crew
revived his damaged heart, we
followed them to the hospital,
summoned family, watched
him wind down. Driving to
his sister, west along the
motorway, clouds edge
red and orange. Look,
the sky, says Ethan,
four, that's grandpa
going up to heaven.

The oldest hatred

Every now and then it makes its way
back, sweeping through air, salmon
swimming upstream, leaping where
required, harder than carbon when
hammered, refusing to yield, close
to truth, swathes feel, more than
logic that deceives by so-called
universal yardsticks from those
old-as-the-hills deceivers; be
firm, folks hate them, no? So
many can't be wrong, you
know it stands to reason,
God or Marx will surely
cast them out, God or
Marx unchoose them.

Inventory

When you reach a certain age, you need
to get beneath the skin of things – poems
prayers, affection, income elasticity in the
service economy, how to slice celeriac for
an even golden look, the heart of matters
few seem to agree on – or simply learn to
let them go, knowing they've eluded you,
time to walk away, to leave, delete, burn
the scorecards, finish, done, other fish
are waiting to be battered, fried; not
to be dramatic, just quietly retreat;
those unexplained conundrums
will find you if they need to;
believe me, they know
where you live.

Coffee united

When, as an encore, Kris Kristofferson sings
Help me make it through the night, he is not
addressing coffee, though it might be in the
back of his mind; in 1553, or thereabouts,
however, Rabbi David ben Solomon ibn
Abi Zimra, also known as the RadBaz,
issued a responsa, likely penned in
Egypt, that coffee did not break
any rules, given how it helped
you study Torah, focus late
into the night. Meanwhile
in 1524, the Grand Mufti
Mehmet Ebuusud el-Imadi
also known as El-İmâdî, issued
a fatwa that the beverage could
be imbibed, similar reasons applying.
I like to think if circumstance ever threw
the two together, one of them to overcome
the first few awkward moments of unexpected
intimacy would, to break the ice, have started with
that.

Last word

Sometimes you have to coax a poem
out of the shadows with a promise
of change and the patience of a
saint; other times, it's ahead of
you, hot to trot, waiting by the
door for your final approval,
just wanting to be sure its
face is clean, its socks
match and it doesn't
have egg on its tie.

Sulphur

Been famous for a time, this fifth
most common element, brimstone
in the bible, though no great shakes
alone, back of the parade, its bolder
sulphide progeny giving off a whiff,
challenging the senses. Elsewhere
on the outskirts, gracious sulphate
siblings ferry joy to junior chemists
gazing down with test tube pride;
tiny homemade clumps of blue
sparkle down the decades.

My room

was dark blue, single bed In the far corner,
desk by the window, burglar-barred like all
the windows, homework, poems (sad to my
mother's chagrin), letters to camp friends,
light blue airmail paper, Khalil Gibran flies
back and forth, populates our margins;
looking out on guava trees, branches of
green mango; portal for the Persian cat
living mostly on the roof, sharing with
successive mongrels clearly not an
option, built-in cupboard on the left
opposite the bookshelves, basin,
mirror by the outside door. I own
that room, that there and then,
though bricks, plaster, paint
and taps have more than
once changed hands
owned for life, on no
map and these
days rarely
visited.

We have no names

Broken days with care can often be repaired,
years are tough and decades tougher now
we have no names, names lost for mingled
bones in forest graves not far outside the
village, for stones or walls, we have no
names, no names for the fishmonger,
teacher, cobbler or chemist, for the
farmer, the market gardener, who
will tend, who will scythe? Maybe
we can make a plan, while soil
does its soft work, melding,
blending, borders fade to
field grass, picnics in the
sun, bread, fruit, honey.

Hello!

All our agents are assisting other
customers, but please hold, your
call is important to us; believe me
we know how you feel; life has its
demands, there are several tasks
on your list today, most of which
will not get done, urgent as they
seem, those seeds of frustration
lining up to germinate, not all our
fault, you'd agree, so please hold,
your call is important to us; I mean
how do you think we feel having to
repeat this again and again when
you know that all our agents are
busy assisting other customers,
even if it's true there may well
be one or two on lunch break
or lingering in the loo, angry
birds on their phone? But
please hold, your call is
important to us. You
don't believe me?
Okay then,
fuck off.

In time

When you don't like what you're hearing,
muscles react, smiles tighten, nothing
you can do. Still, best keep your trap
shut, let it pass, let life head you off,
hi ho Silver, ride into the valley,
kick up new dust; that too
will settle soon enough,
high as it may rise,
hard as hooves
may pound.

At the end of the day

Fear no more the heat
of the sun, suffer with a smile
the relief of shared defeat.

Lope across the street,
promise to go the extra mile,
fear no more the heat.

Give yourself a treat,
accept - resist temptation of denial -
the relief of shared defeat.

Pluck the notes or beat
the drums, solemnise in style,
fear no more the heat.

May the judge's tone be sweet
should the jury quit the trial,
the relief of shared defeat

May our leavings all be neat
though we lurch in single file,
fear no more the heat
the relief of shared defeat.

A day can turn on a dime

It's funny how a day can turn on a dime;
one minute you're lying on a hotel bed
listening to music, preparing for a nap,
next thing you know some bomb in a
random latitude rips faces off the
wrong people; while such who
chose the spot, assembled,
measured, set the clock,
preserve their human
traits, follow teams,
hum when needed
a lullaby or two
for a moment's
peace when
the crying
stops.

Reconciliation

Sometimes numbers refuse to add up,
though you try to drag them back and
forth from one dull column to the next,
sometimes numbers take their stand,
shall not be moved, not be bought,
refuse to come to the table, like
that once close friend going to
their grave, indignant, mad,
unreconciled, ancient
grievance burning,
satisfyingly
intact.

A father's advice

You're closer to the corner than you think;
soon, choices will need to be made, best
keep your eyes peeled, watch the road,
check for the unexpected coming up
on the inside lane; consider all your
options, if less than certain what
to do, to turn or not to turn, just
fake it, look determined; when
others scowl or remonstrate,
rise to the occasion, make
the crudest gesture you
know, curse, Greek or
Afrikaans is best;
this above all, to
thine own self
be forgiving,
these few
precepts
be your
guide.

Common assumption

Staring out at humans on this grey, if mild,
morning, sharing Clapton Common with
the seagulls, geese, a dog or two, one
grey squirrel quivers on a thin bare
branch, and, having seen enough,
forfeits her high station, darts
down and out of sight, some
other place to be, business
to take care of, knowing
reverie is for the birds.

Uncompleted Kaddish

Glorified and sanctified be His great name
'Out, out, out, out!'
throughout the world which He has created
according to His will.
We were shocked,
May He establish His kingdom in your lifetime
and during your days,
we didn't know what was going on, where we are,
and in the life of the entire House of Israel, soon;
we saw only SS with dogs
and let us say, Amen.
and we saw in the distance symmetric lights–
May His great name be blessed forever and to all eternity.
thousands of lights.
Blessed and praised, glorified and exalted,
Out we came from these wagons
extolled and honoured, adored and lauded be
and we had to line up,
the name of the Holy One, blessed be He,
and there were people with striped uniforms.
beyond all the blessings and hymns,
I asked one of them, 'Where are we?'
praises and consolations that are ever spoken in the world;
and let us say, Amen
Without looking at me he said,
May there be abundant peace from heaven, and life, for us
'Auschwitz.' ...
and for all Israel;
'What is Auschwitz?'"
and let us say, Amen.

The music of trees

Not composed for human ears,
diminuendo of mild winter, tone
poem in dawn wind, crescendos
avoided where possible, written
rewritten, performed at random,
rarely repeated as well we know.
Dogs can hear it though; they
show appreciation, moving
tree to tree in their own
time-honoured way.

Back in the day

Despite themselves, they brought it out,
alone, at functions, each in their own
time, the scratched and dented past,
wheels intact; in those days, things
were built to last, the oiled engine
purrs, sounds like new, serviced
as required, stress on innards
more than sheen, sound over
sight, a love, a marriage, we
watched them fight behind
closed doors like cats and
dogs like all their friends
to wall a home, diffuse
the light, to set things
whole, to get it right.

Sometimes

Sometimes things don't add up,
salmon swim downstream to spawn,
silver leaves unfurl to green, black is
whiter than white, sometimes uncles
are not crazy, wicked types do good
deeds, judgment suspended, think
this, vote that, nothing written out
of the script, raindrops land on
cracked ground bouncing into
shape. At some point in your
days to come two plus two
will equal five, you wait,
you'll see, you'll not
believe your eyes.

Missing

Last night we lost an hour; where it went,
who knows? Wasn't there when we woke
up. We'd organise a search, bring some
method to the exercise, but these days
for good reason we're staying indoors.
Early blossoms out braving the cold
work to keep our spirits up. I say
be patient, do your best not to
worry; sooner than you think,
none too worse for wear, it
will find a way back, tail
wagging, asking to be
fed, shivering a little.

Who knows One?

Who knows One? I know One, One is
a father who worked a white desk and
sang if he could, One is the nurse back
on the ward, the new violist, first to go,
One is the helper away from home, One
the joker from down the pub, One is the
neighbour, who seemed nice enough,
One the youngest, laughing by the
fence, One the cleaner, One the
anaesthetist, Who knows One?
I know One, silent on the wire,
repertoire exhausted, I know
One, in the heavens, in the
heavens and on the earth.

While

While we were gone, the
world took a turn, lay down to
catch its breath; in, out.

While we were gone, we
noticed more: the paints, pictures,
fabric of others.

The sun still shone to
keep itself warm and new leaves
unfurling. While we

were gone, our days did
their best to put us at rest,
opened the window,

turned down the volume; welcome,
they said, make yourself at home.

Daily

We have many ways of looking at death;
absolute numbers an easy one, though
tougher when zeroes stack up; another
is deaths per million, changing who's
on top; then by name: Elbert, Habib,
Laura, Areema, each in place along
the graph, together to flatten the
curve, signal success; of course,
there are some who choose to
die of what we know as co-
morbidities; not what we
need to lock the digits
down; but our hearts
go out to them too;
thank you, we'll
now move on
to questions.

The impact of public holidays on productivity in the United Kingdom in the early 21st Century

Even if we can't go out
a change is as good as a rest
a day off is without a doubt

a tonic, makes us feel blessed
our dreams a tad less creased
reins released or loosely held lest

we think we've tamed the beast
that bellows through our working life
for now that noise has ceased

you cut the silence with a knife
thoughts subside, no angry sighs nor
signs of stifled doubt rife

with unresolved belief, inchoate roar,
wanting less, demanding more.

Nearer

Life is nearer the surface these days
skins have thinned; as well to be
indoors. Words stripped back,
shock and awe greet Spring
in mid-stride, blossoms,
now browning, give
way; we thank
them for all
their hard
work.

Restoration

Before this all started, I came across a
bag of words, open, abandoned as if
thrown out in a strop, parts of speech
chocked up willy-nilly, now spilling
out for the world to trample.

I've done what I can, knocked out dents,
sanded down the scratches, wiped off
sludge, picked the ingrained flecks of
grit from cracks and corners, one or
two expletives sadly past repair.

I've hung them out again; feel free to
rummage, some may come in handy
to whomever, salvage hunters, crazy
hoarders, odd collectors, patience
rewarded in our throwaway days.

Do you

ever find yourself before a mirror, shaving,
for example, or glancing in passing at your
own reflection as you amble to the kitchen
for a fresh mug of tea and a biscuit, when
clearly staring back you see a member of
the family, peering through your own eyes
at how you're getting on? First your gran,
then your old man, faces etched into your
own, likeness in a scowl, smile in a twist
of the mouth. We've given you our skin
to grow old in, wear it as you wish,
we'll hold back our advice,
useful as we think
you'd find it.

Someone wrote a book

called This is your Brain on Music that I've
long been meaning to read, but haven't got
round to buying. Perhaps it's all to the good,
brains being fickle that way, one moment in
rapture, fingers making Liszt sound so easy,
reeling you in; then, at the tollbooth, Buddy
Guy, not letting you through without good,
sad reasons; or waking with an ear-worm
you wish had never seen the light of day,
yummy yummy yummy, I've got love in
my tummy, remember that? I've read
there was even music in the Camps,
choirs, orchestras, Glenn Miller for
the inmates, Greig and Mozart for
the guards on Sunday afternoon;
the programme was subject to
change; strings were cut, of
course, the lineups varied.

Instruments are not my friends

Those instruments are not my friends; some defeat
me just by being; others reel me in; hook hurts, they
watch me wriggle and thrash. Worst are ones I've
always thought were friends, various guitars, my
jumbo fan of Leonard Cohen, survivor of a Paris
flood, unpacked soft wood mandolin, glued by
my own hand, unplucked; they beg me raise
them up, berate me my neglect, then out of
spite, defy my scales, confuse my fingers,
dare me try the piano if I think I can do
better. Well what do you expect, they
say, you only ever play that stuff we
know you mastered years ago when
effort was repaid, parents prayed
you'd cut your hair, shirt knotted
for a bucket of dye and battles
were still to be fought and lost;
but listen, here's one you may
remember, it goes a bit like
this.

Zimbabwe dreaming

Sounds like metal rain on an intercity bus
we don't know how to play it, but it knows
how to play us; it's the recollection shuffle
we might even hum along, substitute our
stories for what's really going on.

How long is a piece of string?
A compendium of debates

Compiling this has not been easy. Many
hedge their bets; is or should be, they ask;
a number take the view they can't commit
until they're told what you're trying to do:
wrap a gift or a Sunday roast? tie up one
or two loose ends? For these, one metre
fifty-five would be my guess, I can't be
sure; some go by more or less, thumb
and finger gauge the task; foreswear
precision tools, but mostly, we make
do with random strands or, ball in
hand, cut what we need or what
we can; don't expect the thrill
of the new; page by page it's
more a slog to get through
than a race, but at least
it's here, the whole sad
story, fixed, thorough,
in one place, folded,
trimmed, bound,
who knows,
for glory.

Lazy

Towards the end of a lazy day, the
weekend wind suddenly rose as if
disturbed mid-sleep from a deep
and strange dream, not bad, but
far from sweet, scenes vying for
attention, none with any merit,
weekend wind taking time to
shake them off, settle back
down, alert at last to this
ragged Sunday's final
few possibilities.

Weather report

Capable of more
than this; substantial room for
improvement. Come on!

Eye to eye

We may not all see eye to eye on whether
government is working magic or making a
hash of it, even less on what they should
do next, rows, quite heated, could break
out, brittle insults hurled in the heat of
the moment hard to dismiss after the
fact; but ask this crowd to taste your
soup, tell you what's missing, what
you could add to strike a perfect
balance and new alliances form;
remember whom you looked in
the eye, whom you stood with
on that day, hardly believing.

Surprising what we get used to

First was the hair, follicles deciding
for themselves they need more room
to breathe, losing interest in the common
good, no longer all for one and one for all
then the eyes choosing where to focus,
leaving it at that, restless in the face
of correction; now the skin has its
own ideas, cultivates landscapes;
the ears I believe will be next in
line; of course, I can still hear
fine, even if I don't always
listen.

As a general rule, I don't write about writing but

A semi-famous poet who merits to be
better known once said poems should
open the door, invite you in, then the
door can be closed; and poems may
be sparked by lack of focus, staring
out the window, weather permitting.
He said that too, more or less. I'd
like to state for the record that in
these past few months I've spent
many hours of most days staring
out the bedroom/study window,
door behind me closed. It may
or not have done some good,
perhaps too soon to tell. For
myself, poetically speaking,
results have been mixed,
but I'm sticking with it
nonetheless, gazing,
staying in, while
the jury's out.

Memory's antibodies

Memory has antibodies for outcomes it thinks
might seek a second act, doesn't want to be
the killjoy, lets them loose on what it sees as
suspect cells, leaves the vision more or less
intact, not precious about the frame, going
to work on feelings, soundtracks; how else
could mothers give second birth, soldiers
raise a second weapon, how else to deal
with new love, new grief; it's good at this
is memory, antibodies enter when we're
otherwise engaged, soothing us we're
not on shaky ground, a green light for
an addled brain. "Now won't come
again" is wrong, it's passionate
for encores, clad in different
colours, softer fabrics, us
off-guard, antibodies at
the border, waiting for
orders.

Reckonings

One day they'll be next on the agenda,
other business being concluded; poorly
prepared, made to stand, whom before
as yet unclear, trousers moist on live TV,
reputations sliding as they try to set the
record straight, helping us to grasp the
sacrifice they made, struggling quietly
for change from the inside. Some will
be forgiven, some cast out to scrub,
sins unbalanced, weighing on the
ribs, hooves sinking; names as
footnotes to the final tally,

Hamlet's masterclass

I've witnessed bad decisions shaped in
anger, some my own, which is okay; we
all have those days; the problem comes
with execution; some say strike when the
iron is hot, my take is, better not, it can't
hurt to think again, show patience for the
moment; don't hesitate to hesitate, what
might seem tardy is but thorough; hold
back, trust me, blind thrusts rarely
bring the best results. Next week:
how not to overthink or maybe
something else, depending.

A divine response to theodicy (haiku)

Those who believe that
suffering has a purpose
are clutching at straws.

History of the jigsaw

The master map engraver, who, in 1762, fixed
his world to wood, cut round nations, made a
tool for teachers, deserves some recognition;
no fault of his, the time now spent in private
quests, seekers after missing pieces, even
less the ones whose search is done, those
who hawk the shapes they fashioned, fit
to this or that life puzzle, those who
crisscross streets, lusting after
lost souls, whole stories told,
judgment at one remove;
impatient with our days,
they roam the earth.

August

Gazing off work at the huddles
of leaves on high thin branches
of the common trees outside our
window, mostly plane, welcoming
a heavy rain, grown to block the
occasional pain of the London
sun, I spot the early adopters
making the case for autumn,
shifting gears from science
to art, persuasion starts,
here at the heart at the
heart of the heart.

What next?

Undetermined date,
an afternoon's lazy mood
as memory lies in wait.

Ancient hands knot and bait
the arrow-end for summer's blood;
much begins when it's late.

They rip the night, push the day's gate
shut, the fading light, multi-hued
As memory lies in wait.

The many roads from hope to hate
erode in lonely twilight interlude;
much begins when it's late.

After silent pain, a state
of grace; what else to include
as memory lies in wait?

We line up for the great
renewal, history reviewed,
Much begins when it's late
As memory lies in wait.

This is what it must be like

This is what it must be like to be retired,
leaving the flat to take out the rubbish
and recycling, assuming the bins have
room, Bondi Vet until the time comes
to rise from the chair, reheat coffee,
read the news you just heard on
TV, hoping for an extra fact or
two, distracted by Scrabble,
played when it must be
played, eyes on the
clock, in case you
forget to do that
thing you just
forgot.

Why must the sky be blue?

Why must the sky be blue for us
to thrill? Yes, gold or red with pink
polka dots would just be showing
off, but grey tries hard to please
and does it alone, boasts no deal
with the sun.

Why must the sky be blue for us
to raise a smile, coax our eyelids
closed, dream of meadows and
lawn grass, fresh green rising to
the nostrils, buzz of silence to
uncupped ears.

Let's for once champion the grey, make
it proud to pack its tent and call it a day.

Out of shape

We don't yet have the data, they say,
and if they had the data, then what?
We ourselves have muckles of that
stuff, piling up unfiltered, clogging
cells which might be put to better
use, algorithms foundering, our
obsolescent formulae leading
them astray. If only we had
data we could bank, they
say, we'd set the amber
flashing, try to rein you
in; not that you've a
record of listening
when we do; let's
be honest, said
and done, what
do you think
we're for?
at times
we really
don't know
why we bother.

9/2020

As we speak, a black butterfly
is resting on our bathroom wall,
wings quite still, a respite from
the wind; outside green on grey,
an English way to hint at change,
leaves are paraded, thanked for
efforts to boost the mood; minds
drift, exuberance wanes, shorter
days, advance guard to the chill.
Who knows what else we'll find
when we turn a corner, cloudy
view to winter's edge, thought
unweathered, witnessed from
afar, costumes picked for best
effect, drover of souls, just in
sight, training for his big day.

Being dark outside

Being already dark outside, it is only
when I look towards the street light
I notice it's raining; not with any
great conviction, mind you,
just enough to defend
itself against those
false accusations
of not really
trying, of
dialling
it in.

Glory be

Most of the time, we're head down
trying to get through the day when
every now and then we pull up short
before a miracle. This happens to us
all ~ bakers, driving instructors, even
young technicians in mid-sized towns
with central fountains in need of some
repair ~ a miracle checks our charted
course, yellow bug with golden wings
and red trimming, downfall of a brute,
cheese (most types and flavours) a
certain single malt, vase of flowers,
buds just opened, the first waft of
morning coffee for two; we give
thanks to all these miracles in
our own way, some smile,
some pray, give thanks
to each of these for
suddenly existing,
for drawing the
sting from the
next moment.

Faded ink

Masked up for the moment, waiting
to be summoned, fiddling with the
phone, forcing out the grim news
of the day; plastic teeth are what
we have in store, broken crowns,
acrylic cure. Bite blunted, eyes
dimmed, our fingers still can
trace the faded ink of former
ways; specs removed, we
check both sides, wipe
down lenses, fogged
with aged breath,
the better to see.

Missing in action

Books unopened, letters silent,
fires unfed, sparks unseen, side roads
skipped for want of wonder, hasty
prayers said undeciphered, brittle
copper leaves unraked, root unearthed,
uncooked, unsliced and left to turn,
Kodak film spools undeveloped,
memories of the beach, arguments
remain unsettled, truce unsigned,
GO not passed, updated street
names unrecorded, all the wine
I'll never drink, bottled, labelled,
praises unsung; even so, so
ruby sweet and cool on the lips.

Days

We all have days, awake before our
brain, reset our metronomes in vain,
decry unwelcome shifts from instinct
to choice, silence to voice, jabbing at
familiar buttons, cursing the results,
growling at consequence, flail at
morning's unexplained hostility.
We all have days, next moves
poorly synced, we slip past
ladders, slide down snakes,
throw wrong dice. All of us,
we have such days, don't
we? God, I really hope so.

Why when staring out

Why, when staring out across the common
late damp twilight of a working day, early
London winter in the air, do aged nostrils
reimagine burning grass, yellow-black,
smoke below a fat blue sky, cumulus
sculptures a hemisphere away, foot
on the pedal of a black Rudge bike,
soot specks on a khaki shirt, dry
heat, slow breath, unschooled
In late damp twilights, early
London winters in the air?

Phrases that have recently fallen into disuse

We've just run out of that, I'm afraid
Could you move up a little, please?
It took ages to find a parking spot
Luckily there was a cancellation
Do we really have to go tonight?
If I am not for myself, who will
be for me? and if I am only
for myself, what am I? Try
a sip of mine? And if not
now, when? Great to
see you, come in.
Another glass?
Mmouah,
mouah!

Zimbabwean cento*

Age has taken the blindfold off
And the air is stilled by woodsmoke
A sweet nose-cleansing odour
Laden with promises.

I am still hoola-hooping
Through decades that ran like rivers
The waters unleashed their scything
I get tired of the blood
The ripples are huge
Your wounds will be named silence.

I get tired of the blood
The granite surface of our days
In the mountain mists
Of tumbling kingdoms.

*A cento is a poetical work wholly composed of verses or
passages taken from other authors, especially Homer and
Virgil (though not in this case), in a new form or order
(see below for poets).*

1.	Chigama	8.	Marechera
2.	Eppel	9.	Mungoshi D
3.	Mungoshi C.	10.	Hove
4.	Kabwato	11.	Marechera
5.	Chingono	12.	Hammar
6.	Zimunya	13.	Magadza
7.	Marechera	14.	Magadza

From what I can see

Faced with an imminent winter, local trees
have failed to reach agreement on how to
deal with what's ahead. Some, most even,
stand naked and tall, some prouder than
others; a few are shy to shed, drooping
yellow, defying the odds. while one or
two still signal no intent, on principle
or in denial, move along, they
say, nothing to see here.

Not long ago

Not long ago, we'd calibrate success,
mark how much, how high, how clear,
how far, how firm, how fast; we cleave
now to alternate benchmarks, crises
averted, illnesses overcome, bullets
dodged, lowered sights, victories
of Job. Not long ago, we cheered
at prizes, tears on receipt; we're
thankful since for lack, for little
faults, small mercies, rips in
canvas simply tacked; we
welcome the ragged, the
crinkled, the presently
occluded, somewhat
indistinct, peering
down the road,
embracing for
the moment
the patchy
fog of
limits.

Out the window

At my desk gazing through the window
out across the common; mothers wheeling
buggies stroll into frame, heading north,
chatting, unperturbed by weather; two
clad cyclists pedal south to work or
maybe to the river; all seems right
with their world, they'll deal as
they find. Grandma used to say
we should make the most of
things, that God helps those
who help themselves: also
that her siblings and their
spouses were a bunch of
bladdy shits, though not
when my mother was in
earshot.

At this time of year

At this time of year, some sunsets
are spectacular though they come
too early for my liking; kitchen duties
are a joy, facing west as we do, pinks
lay down a backing for early winter's
brittle copper, warmth, light and soft
relief, a beckoning for hangers on,
reward for faith in who knows
what, prize for last believers.

The political economy of tango in the 21st Century

Percussionists thrive on patience, back
of the orchestra, waiting for a moment,
passion for punctuation tingling in the
bones, not welcome in a Gardel tango,
disrupting the flow with mallets and
hi-hats, when all you want to know
is how it plays out, the ankles flick,
coals smoulder, everything that
happened in the world today,
the price of it all, the lasting
effects to be determined,
not yet important, well
beyond the reach
of melody.

Contractors to the Council

Contractors to the Council are chopping
away the branches that overhang the
road, last leaves having given up the
ghost. Harnessed in guti weather,
orange helmets, yellow jackets,
local Sunday colours, Council
contractors are chopping
branch by dark brown
branch, eyes on the
blade, yesterday's
confabulations
greenly intact.

I don't want to spoil your day, but...

I'm here to tell you that, while impressive,
the hills are not that old, parrots generally
are no sicker than weasels, toast may be
warm in its initial stages, but is far from
efficacious at retaining heat, especially
this time of year; Larry is, for the most
part, not effusively happy, nor, in his
time, was Croesus, despite his lack
of money worries; nails are known
to bend when hammered and the
president of the large Mid-West
Ox Drovers Association is on
record insisting oxen are as
smart as dogs. You're right
about one thing: the grass
is indeed greener on the
other side, though quite
how long it's been so
is anyone's guess.

The butcher (found poem)

When you grow up a kid in a
butcher's house, what your
father brings home at the
end of the day is not the
sirloins, not the filets, it's
pieces and parts, names
rarely uttered, customers
don't ask; I wore an apron,
worked with cleavers for my
sins, before my teeth met steak,
it was okay, the sirloin and filet, It
was okay, it was okay, it was good.
But my grandmother's dishes, were
paradise.

Abraham

Where did Abraham destroy his father's idols?
In his father's shop in Ur of the Chaldees.
When did Abraham destroy his father's
idols? Sometime during shopping hours.
Why did Abraham destroy his father's
idols? He thought they were a con,
didn't pass the smell test. And
how did Abraham destroy his
father's idols? He smashed
the crap out of them with
a stick.

Where did Abraham negotiate with God?
Not far from the terebinths of Mamre.
When did Abraham negotiate with
God? When he heard about the
plan for Sodom and Gomorrah.
Why did Abraham negotiate
with God? Maybe he had
doubts about collateral
damage; as well as his
family reasons, with
his nephew and all.
How did Abraham
negotiate with
God? He used
a what-if
strategy.

Where did Abraham feel bound to sacrifice
his son? Wherever he was when he said,
"Here I am". When did Abraham feel
bound to sacrifice his son? On the
third day of a journey he'd tricked
him into taking. Why did Abraham
agree to sacrifice his son? There
are no good answers. How did
Abraham feel bound to
sacrifice his son? He
followed the rules,
as he knew them.

Where did Abraham sacrifice the ram? There
on the altar he'd readied for his son. When
did Abraham sacrifice the ram? When the
opportunity arose. Why did Abraham
sacrifice the ram? It seemed like a
Godsend. How did Abraham
sacrifice the ram? With the
blade made keen for his
son, multi-hued, if we
believe Chagall.

Why did Abraham bother with the ram? He
didn't want to seem ungrateful; and as for
the ram, caught in the thicket, wrong
place, wrong time, an unexpected
victim in a story not its own, one
it couldn't know, incomplete
down the ages, old knives
already sharpened.